D1742908

CLEVER! CLEVER!
SOMEWHERE! OVER THE RAINBOW
...There's Always Faith & Hope!

CLEVER! CLEVER! SOMEWHERE! OVER THE RAINBOW

...There's Always Faith & Hope!

GLENN LEE

A MARVEL AT THIS! PRODUCTION

This book is a work of fiction. The characters, incidents, and dialogue are drawn from the author's imagination are not to be construed as real. Any resemblance to actual events or persons, living or dead, is entirely coincidental.

CLEVER! CLEVER! SOMEWHERE! OVER THE RAINBOW...There's Always Faith & Hope! Copyright © by Genius In A Bottle Technology Corporation. All rights reserved. Printed in the United States of America. No part of this book may be used or reproduced in any manner whatsoever without written permission except in the case of brief quotations embodied in critical articles and reviews. For information, address Genius In A Bottle Technology Corporation, www.geniusinabottle.net.

Genius In A Bottle books may be purchased for educational, business, or sales promotional use. For information, please email: geniusales@geniusinabottle.net.

CLEVER! CLEVER! SOMEWHERE! OVER THE RAINBOW

...There's Always Faith & Hope!

WRITTEN BY
GLENN LEE

A MARVEL AT THIS! PRODUCTION
2005 © ALL RIGHTS RESERVED

Introduction

Somewhere over the Rainbow,
In My Dark, Dark Sky,
There's a Hero that I dream of,
Way Up High!

With Rainbow Reason,
And Radiant Right,
With Blades of Badness,
And Conceptual Light,

Way Up High,
With Rainbow Reason,
There's a Land where I Live,
Where there's only one Season,

With Rhythmic Energy,
And Renegade Might,
Elemental Powers,
And Boots of Light.

THE SONG OF WEEP

While Walking the Brick,
The Brick of Glory,
A Dilemma! A Dilemma!
In this Strange, Strange Story,

Sat a Strange Moon,
Up in the Sky,
That Haunted Clever! Clever!
As he walked on by,

From out of the Forest,
Searching for Home,
Clever heard a Woman,
With an Enchanting Song,

His eyelids closed,
From The Song of Weep,
Clever! Clever! Fell,
Into a Dark Dark Sleep!

Clever! Clever! Dreamed!
The Dream of Dreams!
About a Land of Darkness!
Where Evil Reigned Supreme!

Once upon a Lullaby,
Way up High,
Sat a Sad Sad Moon,
Up in the Sky,

Where Rainbow Reason,
And Rainbow Right,
Cockatoos nestled,
And Birds of Light,

There's a Land Dreams Enlightened!
Enlightened! Enlightened!
A place where time,
Has surely forgotten.

Chapter One

MYSTICAL STORM

While putting on his sneakers,
Sitting at the table,
Clever's home was taken,
By a Whirling Wild Tornado!

This was not,
An ordinary storm!
Mystical! Mystical Magic!
Began to form!

Caught in a Vortex!
He could not discern,
Ecstatic! Ecstatic!
And the house did burn!

Out of Reality!
And out of touch!
Fire without heat!
There was no such luck!

Like a Comet of Fire,
From out of space,
Came Clever! Clever! Clever!
Through a Three-Dimensional Gate,

A Meteorite Shower!
A Flying Trojan Horse!
No Navigating System!
A Collision! Collision Course!

Like a Comet of Fire!
To the Land of Hate!
Came Clever! Clever! Clever!
From out of space!

The wind was Furious!
The Sky was Dark!
The House lit up Heaven!
Like a Giant, Giant Spark!

Towards a Dark Empire!
Towards a Dark World!
Came Clever! Clever! Clever!
And The House that Swirled!

Out of Time!
With a Heavenly Desire!
Came the Angel of God!
And his Chariot of Fire!

Out of time,
And out of hope!
Came The Hand of God,

Upon the Eastern Slopes!

Spinning from the Hemisphere!
The House did Zoom!
It hit Dark Castle!
With a Sonic, Sonic Boom!

Smite! Smite! Smite!
Crashing through the Hall!
The House nailed the Witch,
Against the Evil Wall!

Was this the Will of Destiny?
Or the Cruel Trick of Fate?
To put him on a World,
Where there was so much Hate,

Smoke filled his lungs,
Dizzy and bothered,
Stumbling out of the Crash,
And this She did Holler!

"Vile Acid Blood!
Seeping From My Heart!"
Clever! Clever! Terrified!
At this Ghastly Wicked Art!

His Heart made of Gold,
He checked her dying pulse,
A last instinctive instinct,
With an Electric Evil Jolt!

He screamed in Horror!
And Fell in Pain!
A Sinister Wicked Deed!
From Evil! Evil Jane!

Losing Reality,
In the Dark Dark Hall,
Stumbling back, back,
And He did fall,

He hit the floor,
With a force so hard,
It knocked Clever out,
Like a deck of Cards,

There they lay,
In the Room of Fate!
A man created by Destiny,
And a Woman Destroyed by Hate!

Startled as he woke,
"What hit me Man?!!"
He looked around the room,
And then at His hands,

The Stone, Stone Tablets!
She held clutched in her hands,
Melted around the wrist,
Of the Genius, Genius Man!

Chapter Two

DARK FOREST

The Creatures in the Hall,
Sang the Song of Hate,
And chased Clever! Clever!
To Forbidden Gate!

Losing his sanity,
But not his mind,
Clever! Clever! Frantic,
And he did climb,

Clever found his way,
Out of the Evil, Evil Hall,
And made his way,
Down Forbidden Wall!

A World of Darkness,
A Land of Hate,
How could Any, Anyone,
Live in this Place?!!

Clever pondered a thought,
How long would it last?
He knew he was the result,
Of an Inescapable Past!

He ran to Dark Forest,
And this he did Zoom,
He flew like the Cow,
Jumping over the Moon.

Out of the Fire,
And into the Pan,
Ran Clever! Clever! Clever!
And the Bracelets of Sand!

The Forest was thick,
Up in the sky!
Thunder-Energy!
Thunder-Energy!
Bolts Up High!

The wind did blow,
And the trees did shutter,
What was that sound?
And this he did utter,

"Up in the Sky,
Sat a Dark! Dark Moon!
Down in the Forest,
Lurked creatures of Doom!"

He came to a clearing,
And what did he see?
A Golden Scarecrow,
Nailed to a tree,

Upon his face,
Pain and Anger,
A Man Made of Straw,
With Redemptive Danger!

Upon His Face!
A Scary, Scary Grin!
A Hypnotic Smile!
And Death Within!

"What is this thing?
This Listening Grin?!!
With the Heart of Shadows!!!
And the Souls of Men!?!!"

The Creatures that sat,
Perched on his shoulder,
This they did chant,
Over and Over!

"If you Let Him down!
He will Destroy!
Beware! The Crow Man!

The Hero of Troy!"
A map in need,
To Navigate the Land,
Clever perplexed,
By the "Sign Post Stand!"

"The Nail! The Nail!
The Nail of Law!
Beware! Beware!
The Man made of Straw!"

Clever saw his anguish,
And Clever felt his pain,
He knew the Golden Nail,
Was the Deadly, Deadly Stain,

The Golden Nail,
Thrust so far,
Clever pulled it out,
Of the Straw Man's Heart,

With an Eerie Scream!
"I'm Free! I'm Free!
Face me Demon!
Who opposes Me!"

Clever! Clever! Clever!
Upon his face,
He saw a vision,
He knew he would hate,

The Golden Straw!
Turned Black! Black! Black!
He knew the Crow Man,
Had The Power to Attack!

Straw Face Black,
Black as tar,
Clever took off,
But didn't get far,

He tripped on fear,
This he would endeavor,
Down to the ground,
Went Clever! Clever! Clever!

With Bitterness and Anger,
In his Heart,
He lashed out at Clever,
From near and far,

Razors of Straw,
Followed this Lad,

Clever looked up,
And he was sad,

In a Quick, Quick Flash,
The Scare Crow zoomed,
Over Clever! Clever!
He did Loom!

The air was filled,
With Straw and Hay,
The Scare Crow made a Vow,
His enemy he would Slay,

"With the Power of Knowledge!
And the Power I Command!
I summon The Power of!
The Scare Crow Man!"

From out of the Forest!
The sound he heard!
A Million! A Trillion!
Crow-Matic Birds!

The Straw took Shape!
Sharp as a saw!
The Scare Crow's Hands!
Turned Killer Claw!!

"Pick His Bones!!!
Pick them Clean!!!
Clever looked up!
And He was Mean!

As he Summoned the Power,
The Power of The Straw,
What do you think,
The Crow Man saw?

Around his wrist??!!
Wait! Wait! Wait!
The boy possesses the stones?!!!
The Power of Fate!!!"

The Scare Crow Astonished!
Total Disbelief!
He asked Himself,
"How could she be beat?!!"

"You there!!
You there!!
Under the Tree!
You are The Answer!
You are The Key!

You are The Riddle!
The Riddle!!!

The Rhyme!!!
You are the Answer!
To These Dark,
Dark Times!"

"Tell me Boy!"
Was the question at hand,
"Tell me Child!
How did you come to this land?"

Clever quickly asked,
Am I your slave?
The Scare Crow looked away,
We have a World to Save!!"

"You are The Reason!!
The Reason and The Rhyme!
You are the Boy!
Of Poetic Time!!!

"Get on your Feet!
And come with me!!
We must journey afar!
To find The Fantastic Three!

Chapter Three

THE WITCH

Back at the castle,
The Castle of Doom,
The Witch arrived,
On Her Magic Broom,

Pointed Hat,
Skin all Green,
Eyes Full of Hate,
Black and Mean,

Garbed in Black,
Nails Long and Sharp,
Nose like a Buzzard,
With a Dark, Dark Heart,

"Who Crucified My Twin?!!
I will atone!
And Where?!! Oh Where?!!
Are the Tablets of Stone??!!!"

The creatures they shuttered,
They shivered and shaked,
Then they told the Witch,
Who had came to this place,

They began to hum,
And started to sing,
They told The Witch of Witches,
Of the Deadly! Deadly Sting!

"It was Clever! Clever! Clever!
And the House of Light!
He killed your sister!
On this Dark, Dark Night!"

The Resident of Evil,
Screamed in pain,
Then she took off,
On her Evil Train,

Up in the sky,
Electricity she hurled,
An Evil Driven Frenzy,
Screamed this Bewitched Bat Girl,

The witch flew away,
She flew away in pain,
She could not stop, stop,
Reciting Clever Clever's name,

"Clever! Clever! Clever!
A Human Toy!
Clever! Clever! Clever!
You're just a Boy!"

"Clever! Clever! Clever!!
Driving me insane!!
Clever! Clever! Clever!!
Let's Bring on The Pain!!!"

As she flew away!
This she endeavored!
"I'll Get You Human!!!
Named Clever! Clever! Clever!

Chapter Four

MAGIC MOUNTAIN

The Scare Crow sensed,
Her Evil, Evil Anger,
A Dark, Dark Scream,
With Punitive Danger,

So up Magic Mountain,
The two did claw,
One Human Boy,
And the Man Made of Straw,

They came to a Cave,
And It did block,
A Mountain, Mountain Man,
That was Made of Rock!

"If you want to go,
And pass within,
Answer this Question,
And how have you been?"

Clever recited,
The poem out loud,
And Heavenly Lighting,

Came from the clouds,

The boy solved The Puzzle!
The "Riddle of the Rock!"
And drove Mountain Man,
Back into his flock!

The Mountain Man returned,
Returned to the rock,
And Crow Man unlocked,
The Secret, Secret Lock!

Clever saw the Power,
And Clever felt the cold,
The Sword of Sadness!
Behold! Behold!

"You cannot possess,
The Sword of Sadness!
Until you Recite,
The Poem of Madness!"

The Sword of Sadness!
To you it will Belong!
The Sword of Swords!
Has a Mind of its Own!

Clever stared at,

The Sword of Sadness!
His Eyes became Thunder!
Thunder and Madness!

He recited The Poem,
"The Sword of Sadness,"
The Cave did Shake!
With Power and Badness!

The Sword did Shimmer!
And it took Flight!
Thunder-Energy! Thunder-Energy!
Bolts of Light!

It did Glow,
In this Dark Cave Place,
Then Vanished! Vanished!
Without a Trace!

Where did it go?!!
"Into the Night!
It can only be summoned,
When there is a Fight!!!"

How do you know?!!
"No one Knows,
Come with me Boy,
The Story Unfolds!

Chapter Five

SILVER FOUNTAIN

The Journey down the Mountain,
Was Fierce and Mean!
The Witch was after him,
A Fiendish Fiend,

At the bottom of Magic Mountain,
What did appear?
A Silver, Silver Fountain!
Oh Dear! Oh Dear!

What do you think,
Was at hand?
But a Mirror Mirror Image,
Of a Frozen Tin Man!

The Water that was Running,
Was Silver and Gold,
The Tin Man began,
To Recite these Odes,

Who can you guess,
Put Me in this State?
Liquid and Light,
Made of Solid Solid Hate!

A Periodic Table!
You can't find in this Room,
Analyze the Questions,
On the Colorful Cards of Doom!

Recite this Message,
Recite this text,
A Canine Friend,
Will Forever Protect,

Add One Value,
To the Number Nine,
And a Frozen Friend in Me,
You will find,

With the Power of Ten,
Around Your Neck,
Freedom from Evil,
I do detect,

Subtract One Value,
From the Number Eleven,
And the Other Other Friend,
You'll find in Heaven,

Subtract One Value,
Before it's too late,
I am the Map!
The Key to Faith!

If you Solve the Riddle,
Of All That Jazz,
I will be a Showman,
Of the Glass! Glass-Class!

If you Solve the Riddle,
Of the Colorful Cards of Doom,
Out of this Table,
I will Zoom!

Scare Crow Man's Patience,
Was Growing Thin,
"Nonsense! Nonsense!
Speaks the Man of Tin!"

I will Destroy!
Destroy this Ridiculous Fountain!!
It will never Trick Us!!!
Who toiled From the Mountain!!

Clever begged the Crow Man,
To leave it alone,
"If you destroy it now!
I may never get home!"

So upon the Table,
Lay Ten Colorful Cards,

Five with Text,
And the other with Stars,

So there they sat,
At the Table of Doom!
Dealt a Decisive Hand,
Pondering under the Moon,

Clever went to the Fountain,
To wash His Face,
And what did he see,
Through the Liquid Water Gate?

At the Stroke of Midnight,
Like the Galactic Eyes of God,
Clever found the Answer,
Up under the Stars,

Knowledge of the Universe,
Roamed His Mind,
Transforming Matter,
Essence and Time,

So Faster that Faster!
Than the Speed of Light!
Could this be the Answer?!!
Would He be right?!!

"I Know! I Know!
Why this Riddle's Absurd!
It was Hidden, Hidden!
And Submerged!

He reached in the water,
And what did he snag?
A Necklace! A Pendant!
No a Dog Dog Tag!

He placed the Amulet,
Around his neck,
And from this moment on,
He recited these text:

"With a Dog Tag Amulet,
Around My Neck!
Power Unleashed,
As I recite these Text!"

"With the Power of Knowledge!
With the Power I Command!
Virtues of Life and Melanin Man!

My Dark Dark Sky!
A Vision that Looms!
I am the Master of,
The Colorful Cards of Doom!"

Out of the Distance,
And into the Night,
Came a Brilliant Brilliant Glow,
And a Burst of Light!

It hit the Fountain,
With a full Power Max!
Appeared before them,
Was a Man with an Ax!

There he stood,
This Silver Man,
A Metallic Mortal,
With an Iron Hand!

A Silver Power,
With a Silver Tan!
Spit-Polish with,
A Salute so Grand!

With Aluminum Skin!
A Hero in a Book!
An Immortal Statue!
With an Eternal Look!

Look up in the Sky!
It's Rain not Sand!
If you count to nine,
It's a Shinny Tin Man!

So the Ten Man said,
Lets be on our way,
He led us to a place,
Where Lions stay,

Chapter Six

EYES IN THE DARK

To lead us through the Land,
Of the Dark Shadows of Hell,
We need the Giant Cat!
With a Keen Sense of Smell!

We went in a cave,
And what was inside?
Glowing in the Dark,
Were two Large Eyes!

A Scary Voice asked,
Has it gone? Has it gone?
A Mouse?!! A Mouse?!!
With two Big Horns!!!

Out of the cave,
Ran a Mouse with a Smile,
The Scare Crow replied,
This Lion's like a child!

The Ten Man said,
We need your help!
The Lion Roared! Roared!

"Find Her Yourself!!"

So you know why we're here,
Before it's too late,
Help us Cowardly Lion,
Find the Woman named Faith!

He came out the shadows,
This Giant Beast!
He looked at Clever,
Like he was a feast!

He walked up to him,
And Clever got scared,
He held out his paw,
And said "Hello there!"

"Do me a favor?
And keep a look out,
Warn me when you see,
That Scary, Scary Mouse,

Everyone laughed,
And told some jokes,
Clever exclaimed,
"He's actually nice to folks!"

They trekked through the Forest!
The Shadows of Hell!
The Lion said "Wait!!
What is That Smell??!!"

Clever lit a match,
And what did they see?
A thousand Winged Monkeys!!!
Hanging from a tree!

The Scare Crow Man Summoned,
The Power of the Crow!
The Lion Roared! Roared!
"You are My Foe!"

We fought them off,
With the **Force of Four!**
And the Ten Man Axed,
One to the floor!

The Bloody Battle was over!
They Fought and Won!
The Lion jumped up!
And said "That was Fun!"

Chapter Seven

THE GOLDEN GLASS CASKET OF FAITH

Hurry! Hurry! Hurry!
We must be on our way!
The War just Begun,
Cause One got Away!

They climbed Castle Wall,
And through Wicked Gate,
Ten Man whispered,
Hurry! Before it's too late!

The Power to stop her,
Is in this room,
They all felt the presence,
Of an Evil, Evil Goon,

We must move the wall,
And enter the gate,
Hurry Now!
Before it's too late!

He chopped through the wall,
And peered at the gate,
Beyond this fence,
Lay the Casket of Faith,

He looked in the hole,
And what amazed me!
The Ten Man used,
His Ax as the Key!

With the Ax of Silver,
He Unlocked the Gate,
Hurry! Hurry! Hurry!
Before it's too late!

In the Golden Glass Casket,
There She lumbered,
A Beautiful Black Woman,
That Slumbered and Slumbered,

Hair of Gold!
Lips embedded Diamonds!
Ruby jewel Nails!
And Eyes of Almond!

"How do we open it?"
"And save this land?"
They whispered "Clever! Clever!"
"Use the Bracelets of Sand!"

Clever held the Bracelets,
The Bracelets of Stone,
He Repeated! He Repeated!

"There's No Place Like Home!"

"This World is out of Hope,
This World is out of Faith,
Release! Release!
The Goddess without Hate!"

Somewhere! Somewhere!
The Belief did Flow,
Clever! Clever! Baptized,
In a Golden Rainbow!

The Glass disappeared!
And Faith took Flight!
She endowed Clever! Clever!
With Boots of Light!

Chapter Eight

THE BEWITCHING HOUR

The Witch appeared!
This Evil Twin!
Lion Flinched! Flinched! Flinched!
To the Cruel Stench of Sin!

She Stared in Hate!
And this She Endeavored!
She shouted out his Name!
"Clever! Clever! Clever!"

The Crow Man Attacked!
With His Crow-Matic Crows!
The Witch waved her hands!
And bewitched them to the floor!

She jumped on her Broom!
And flew in the air!
All we could see,
Was her Deadly Deadly Stare!

"I've been waiting for You!!!
To spring My Trap!
Three Fool! Fools! Fools!!!
And one human sap!!!"

She used Black Magic!
And Hurled it as she Zoomed!
The Tin Man shielded us!
With the Colorful Cards of Doom!

The Lion Leaped!
From Rock to Rock!
He sprang in the air,
Like a wind up clock!

He Slashed at the Witch!
We could hear Her Scream!
He knocked her off,
Her Mean Machine!

She hit the ground!
My Neck! My Neck!
Then she called forth!
A Deadly Hex!

"With the eyes of demons!
From the pits that smell!
Arise demon apes!
From the pits of Hell!!!"

The Castle Wall's Cracked!
And the floor did crumble!
From under our feet!
A Grumble! Grumble!

The Castle Roof Exploded!
And Expelled!
Down from Below!
Came the Apes of Hell!

Trillions! Millions!
Came to Her side!
The Four looked in Horror!
Just Petrified!

"To aid my flame!!!
I call to Dark World!!!
The Wizard of Pain!!!"

The three yelled to Clever!
"Don't stand there Son!"

"We'll try to hold them off!"
"Run! Run! Run!"

The Mighty Lion Roared!
"Die! My Foe!"
Pain hit him hard,
With One Death Blow!

The Crow Man Flung!
His Razors of Straw!
The Witch responded,
With "The Nail of Law!

The Man Made of Ten,
A Last Defense!
He Hurled his Mighty Ax!!
But would it make sense??

Into the Dense!
His Majestic Ax Hailed!
They deflected His Chop!
"Scrap Metal for Sale!"

The Apes took turn,
Slamming their Hands!
They all scattered back,
A Battered Ten Man!

Clever looked around,
Surrounded by Goons!
His Three Friends Down!
And Him with No Room!

The Witch slapped Him down!
And thus began to punch,
Made the Clever Boy,
Throw up his lunch!

The Wizard of Pain!
Blasted His Heart!
Clever hit a tree!
Almost tore Him Apart!

Bruised and Battered!
Battered and Bruised!
Clever looked up,
How did we lose?

His Body all Bloodied!
Beaten and Battered!
He asked Himself!
Why? Why does it matter?!

He could still hear the Witch,
And her Evil Band!
"The Killing Time is Ripe!
And near at hand!!!"

You're in a Bind!!
An evil tether!!
You're going to Die!!!
Clever! Clever!

Relinquish the bracelets!
And the Boots of Light!
And I Promise! I Promise!
To Spare your Life!!

Clever was weary,
And Disdained,
Freedom without Hate!
Was Worth the Gain!

This World has Hope!
This World has Faith!
We have Released!
The Goddess without Hate!

Chapter Nine

THE VOICE FROM WITHIN

His eyelids closed,
Now and forever,
That's when a Voice said,
Clever! Clever! Clever!

He heard a voice,
Down in His Heart,
"There's nothing you can't finish,
Thant you didn't start,"

With Love and Justice,
In His Heart,
Clever found the Faith,
To do his part,

So He closed his eyes,
And said a Silent Prayer,
His Soul transcended,
And rose to the air,

The boy finally understood,
The Riddles of Time,
He began to recite,

His Poetic Rhymes,

"To stop this Evil!
And make things Right!
I Energize My Feet!
With the Boots of Light!!"

"With the Power of Knowledge!
And the Power I Command!
I Summon the Power!
Of the Scare Crow Man!"

The Crow Man's Soul!
A Mysterious Sight!
Battle Armor Ready!
To even the Fight!

The Scare Crow Shape-shifted!
As it did float!
Around Clever's Body!
In a Dark Black Coat!

"Dark Dark Soul!
And Dark Dark Sky!
I Summon the Power!
The Power to Fly!"

His Super Coat!

A Dark Dark Swirl!

Lifted Clever ! Clever! Clever!
Above the World!

So up above!
He acquired the Power!
This Angel of God!
In this moment and hour!

There He stood!
Way up High!
This Dark Dark Man!
In His Dark Dark Sky!

"With the Power of Love!
To End this Madness!
I call upon The Sword!
The Sword of Sadness!"

Cosmic Energy Power!
From the Eyes of this Boy!
Lightning and Thunder!
From the Dark Dark Floor!

The Sword of Sadness!
In the Night!

A Dark Holy Rapier!
Born of Chaotic Light!

The Sword of Sadness!
Did appear!
The Demons Panicked!
And They did Fear!

"I Wield The Sword!
The Sword of Sadness!
It has The Power!
Of Destructive Madness!"

Up in the Heavens,
Clever did Behold,
The Power of Faith,
And His Dark Dark Soul!

Somewhere over the Rainbow!
In My Dark, Dark Sky,
There's a Hero that I dream of,
Way Up High!

With Rainbow Reason,
And Radiant Right,
With Blades of Badness,
And Conceptual Light,

Way Up High,
With Rainbow Reason,
There's a Land where I Live,
Where there's only one Season,

With Rhythmic Energy,
And Renegade Might,
Elemental Powers,
And Boots of Light.

A Lullaby, Lullaby,
Clever did find,
He recited a secret,
From the Scrolls of Time,

An Unspoken Ode,
From Delilah's Avenger,
Clever became,
God's Poetic Dark Defender!

The Clay He Shaped,
It did Inspire,
Light from His Hands,
Spoke the Phoenix of Fire!

"Clever! Clever! Clever!

Holds the Sword of Sadness!
And I Wield the Power of,
"The Blades of Badness!"

The Phoenix of Fire!
Created this Lad,
No longer Clever! Clever!
But Clever Super Bad!

Out of the Ashes!
Rose Not a Toy!
Clever Super Angered!
A Mighty Battle Boy!

Resonating Power!!!
Vortex Chamber!!!
Blades of Badness!!!
And Redemptive Danger!!!

With The Power of God!
In His Hand!
Clever! Clever! Clever!
A Forever Man!!!

In His Heart!

He did Find!
The Power of Peace!
A Forbidden Rhyme!

The Secrets of Secrets!
From The Ancients of Time!
The Secrets of Secrets!
A Poetic Rhyme!

Summoning Holy Power!
From The Dark Dark Sky!
The Arc of All Angels!
God's Poetic Eye!

"With a Dog Tag Amulet,
Around my neck,
Power Unleashed!
As I recite these text!

With the Power of Knowledge!
And the Power I Command!
Virtues of Life,
And Melanin Man!

My Dark Dark Sky!
A Vision that Looms!
I am the Master!
Of the Colorful Cards of Doom!

With the Sword of Sadness,
In my hand!
Banish these Demons,
From this Dark Dark Land!!!

With The Power of Dark!
With The Power of Love!
I Call Forth The Power!
From High Up Above!

With The Sword of Sadness!
In My Hand!
And the Power of God!
At My Command!

I command the Heavens!
And Faith without Sin!
Destroy! Destroy!
This Diabolical Twin!

Faster than Faster!
Than the Speed of Smite!
Out of Heavens!
Came The Boots of Light!

Out of The Vortex!
Clever did Zoom!
Over the Witch,
He did Loom!

He heard the Witch,
And this she endeavored,
"Mercy on me,
Clever! Clever! Clever!"

He held the Lightning Rod!
With Vengeance and Madness!
Lightning from the Heavens!
Sung the Blade of Badness!

He looked at the Heavens!
And peered in Her Eyes!
He saw the Face of Truth!
And the Long Look of Lies!

He Finally Got the Chance,
To Do His Part!
As He pulled The Sword of Sadness,
Out of the Dying Witch's Heart!

When the Dust had cleared,
And the Smoke was gone,
Clever found Himself,
All Alone,

The Last One Standing,
His Friends in His Soul,
Clever to Himself,
The Light of Gold?!!

I haven't a Clue,
And I'm All Alone,
I'm not really sure,
How to get back home,

Clever! Clever! Clever!
You always had the Power to go home,
You just had to Believe,
In the Power of Your Own,

Clever asked Faith,
Will I see you again?
"Not in the World,
Of the Promised Land!"

Faith wished him luck,
As She flew from here,
Tears from Her Eyes,
As She disappeared,

Her Tears hit the Pavement,
With a Brilliant Light!
The Land went from Darkness,
To Golden Yellow White!

Clever gaze,
Upon an Amazing Sight!
A World Full of Faith,
And Beautiful Sunlight!

It Inspired his Heart,
With a Wonderful Desire,
The Answer to Home,
Faith Truly Inspired,

He raised His Sword,
And a Rainbow Appeared,
Lightning and Thunder,
From the Stratosphere!

He recited a Poem,
In a Rhythmic Text,
And Clever disappeared,
Through a Black Vortex...
...Somewhere over the Rainbow.

The End

The Forever Four!
Clever! Clever!
Meets Battle Girl
And the Staff of Power

Chapter One

BATTLE GIRL SUMMONS BATTLE BOY

Battle Girl! Battle Girl!
And her Quiet Power,
Beautifully equipped,
With a Deep Down Desire!

She's in a bind!
An Evil Tether!
She needs the power
Of Clever! Clever!

In a cave,
She did find,
The Stone, Stone Tablets,
And the Text of Time!

She recites the words,
With her Lips of Passion,
"Bring me The Man!
The Sword of Sadness!"

Lightning from the heavens,
Came to the floor,
"Who calls The Power
Of Battle Boy?!!

With Eyes of Love,
She looked up high,
And down he came,
From the Dark Dark Sky!

She did behold,
A Magnificent Sight!
A Man of Dark!
An Omnipotent Knight!

Born of The Cosmos,
A Friend of the Weather,
"I'm Clever! Clever!
And I'm Stronger than Ever!

Out of control,
Up higher, higher,
Clever felt The Burn!

The Ultimate Fire!

His Eyes full of Lightning!
His Coat a Dark Swirl!
Why did you summon me?!!
Battle Girl?!!

I wield the sword!
The Sword of Sadness!
It has the Power!
Of Dark Dark Madness!

Why did you call me,
My Dark Dark Pearl?!!
Why did you summon me?!!
Battle Girl?!!

She stared and asked,
Are you and the stars related?
He looked at Heaven,
"No! It's complicated!"

What is your relationship,
With the Heavens and the Stars?
He looked at the sky and said...
"I'm Unfound by Mars!"

"I'm just a Man,

Known as Clever! Clever! Clever!
A Poetic Sentient walking
The Brick of Forever!"

What is your Origin?
Where is your home?
"I was created from,
A Dark Dark Poem!"

"A Diamond in the Rough,
Neither a million nor zero,
I am what you call,
A Tragic! Tragic Hero!"

"I hold in my hand,
To Heal this Madness,
The Power of Love!
And The Sword of Sadness!"

"My Blood is Pure!
Lightning is My Soul!
My Eyes of Thunder!
My Heart of Gold!"

"In the Mist,
Of the Mystical Hurricane Night,
I will do Battle!
And Fight! Fight! Fight!"

"In the Mist,
Of the Mystical Hurricane Night,
I stand Alone!
This Dark Dark Knight!

"So you ask me a Question,
You Ponder my Soul,
With the Heart of a Champion,
My Story Unfolds!"

"You Riddle Me a Question,
You Query my Soul,
My eyes filled with Love,
And My Tears Untold!"

Chapter Two

The Universe Calls,
And beckons Me near,
The evil within you,
I Fear! Fear! Fear!

"With the Carnage of Dark Angel,
And Eternity's Eyes!
Battle Girl! Battle Girl!
Where is your smile?"

"Somewhere over the rainbow,
My Heart does Sing,
I felt the Love,
Of your Forgotten Sting!"

With the Love of Dark Angel,
My Heart knows no fear,
Bring back the Love,
Of your Abandoned Tear!

He gazed at Her Soul,
And peered in Her Eyes,
He saw the Face of Truth,
And the long Look of Lies!

"The Evilest of Evil,
Has tainted Your Soul,
A Spirit now Rotten,
Of Mildew and Mold!"

"It has Cursed Your Spirit,
And Violated your Soul,
Sanity and Conscience,
You're unable to hold!"

Take my hand,
In this moment and hour,
And together we will defeat,
This Dark Dark Power!

She placed her hand,
In the Palm of Power,
And together Baptised,
In a Dark Rainbow Shower!

So Up to Heaven,
With Ulysses' Bow!
And Down to Hell,
With a Halo!

This place is not new!
Tarnished and old!
Clever to Her,
We are in your Soul!

Chapter Three

EVIL APPEARS

Then out of the Darkness!
At the Speed of Smite!
An Evil Vile Substance!
Caught the Man of Light!

It whipped and latched him,
To An Unholy Door!
Then Evil manifested,
From the Dark Dark Floor!

Clever to himself,
What is this Dark Thunder?!!
With the Power of Terror,
And the Might to Plunder!

What is this Essence?!!
This Listening Grin?!!
An Evil Awaits!
In The Shadows of Sin!

Clever drew in his head,
Half-dazed, and Half-conscience,
Up It came like
An Abominable Man-Monster!

What did the horror,
Of their eyes did appear?
Death's Door Doorman,
Carrying Deadly Gear!

From out of the shadows,
His eyes pierced my soul,
His gaze like a snake,
And his stare was so cold,

Drenched in blood,
From its head to its feet,
Its fangs were all tarnished,
With darkness and deceit,

From the crack of its mouth,
It let forth a dark grin,
Its voice filled the room,
Like a horrible sin,

Chained and racked,
Whipped to a stutter,
I barely heard his words
And this it did utter,

"Make yourselves at home,
While we tear at your flesh,
I am your host,

And you are my guest!

Tonight we will dine,
On rot and insects,
And my minions from the depths,
Will devour the rest!

Clever to you,
I am the Dark Master!
Take him! Destroy her!
Death and Disaster!

From the Eyes of Heaven,
An Unspeakable Hell!
They slithered toward her,
This Battle Girl!

Battle Girl's body,
A Human Cargo-casket,
To enslave her soul,
A Merciless Mid-Passage!

Chapter Four

BATTLE GIRL'S DEFENSE

Battle Girl! Battle Girl!
And The Staff of Power,
Tattoo on Her Skin,
Of a Flutter, FlutterFlower,

An Elemental Woman,
With a body that rocks,
Chains around her hips,
Hung a ChatterBox,

She held in her hand,
The Staff of Power,
An Elemental Woman,
A Beautiful Black Flower!

Eyes of Almond,
She could see the Danger,
An Evil Evil Presence!
With a Dark Dark Anger!

With Creative Energy,
And Radiant Light,
Battle Girl knew,
It was time to Fight!

Clever! Clever! Bound,
He could do not a thing,
Helpless as he watched,
And she did sing,

Chapter Five

Energized Power! Cosmic Tongue!
She began to Chant an Elemental Song!

He never would have imagined,
As he watched her sing,
Out from her mouth,
Came a FlutterFly Thing!

Energized too,
A Maximum Load!
FlutterFly released
A FlutterFly Fold!

This Magnificant Rift,
An Amazing Sight!
A Beautiful Dark Power!
With Radiant Light!

Death was contained,
But would it hold?!
Trapped and imprisoned,
Inside a FlutterFold!

Battling their onslaught,

She had to kneel,
Protected! Surrounded!
A Flutter Force-Field!

This was a lesson,
Clever did behold,
She energized her Bubble,
With FlutterFly Gold!

Seeds of Doom
Was the Mask of the Hour,
Up from below,
Came FlutterFly Flowers!

With the Wisdom of Egypt!
With the Destruction of Time!
She began to recite,
An Elemental Rhyme!

"With the Power of a Nzinga!
With the Wisdom of a Fox!
I Summon to Battle!
My ChatterBox!"

The Light of Redemption
Flowed from the Lock!
Burning and Searing
Spoke the ChatterBox!

Clever beheld,
An Enchanting Sight
Battle Girl Power!
Battle Girl Might!

The Lock of Locks!
It did Swirl!
Out from The Box!
Came a ChatterBox Girl!

She released a Chatter!
She released a Sound!
She dealt a blow,
To the Hells of Hound!

It's Time! It's Time!
It's Time to leave!
I Destroy you Monsters!
With ChatterBox Speed!

She had a need!
To release the Power!
Emitted Chatter Sound!
An Angelic Rainshower!

Drops of Honey,
Intrinsic Heaven Dew!
It drenched and changed them,

Into Devil Goo!

Fighting for her Soul,
Against Death and Disaster!
FlutterFly! ChatterBox!
But this did not matter!

Low on Redemption,
And Universal Sight!
She held her own,
But she was losing the fight!

Chapter Six

CLEVER UNLEASHED

With love and redemption,
In his heart
There was nothing he couldn't finish,
That he didn't start,

"With Eternity's Eyes!
And Infinity's Flower!
I am the Master!
Of The Boots of Power!"

His Boots emitted,
Radiant Light!
Clever! Clever! Knew,
It was time to fight!

He stared at His Boots,
And looked at the sky,
Then called forth,
The Power to Fly!

"I am Clever! Clever!
To end this madness,
I call upon The Sword!
The Sword of Sadness!!!"

Lightning from the Heavens
Came to the floor,
It transformed Clever
Into Battle Boy!

The Sword of Sadness!
In the night,
Thunder-Energy! Thunder-Energy!
Bolts of Light!

Arching Bolts of Lightning!
Came to this Man!
It came from The Rapier!
Right to his Right Hand!

Teleported Knife!
The Sword of the Hour!
Appeared before Clever!
Now He had the Power!

Clever's Sword Handle,
With the Hand of More,
And thrust the Long Dagger
Right to the floor!

His Super Coat!
A Dark Dark Swirl!
Lifted Clever! Clever!

Above the World!

There He Stood!
Way up High!
This Dark Dark Man,
In a Dark Dark Sky!

"I am the Master!!
I am the Master!
I am the Destroyer!
Of Death and Disaster!

I now know why,
The Cage Teacher Sings!
She has felt the Filth!
And the Lash of Ming!"

Chapter Seven

THE FOREVER FOUR

"Demon Demon!
I could not before!
I Now Wield The Power!
The Power of Four!

Heed My Command!
And free the Black Flower!
You will Release Battle Girl!
This Day! This Hour!"

"With the touch of my Amulet,
I Unlocked the Lever!
Come stand by Clever! Clever!
Now and Forever!"

With the Courage of the Lion!
My Heart knows no Sin!
I call forth The Power!
The Power of Ten!

With the Power of Ten!
With the will of Iron!
I call forth the Strength!
The Courage of The Lion!

With the Love of Dark Angel!
I stand before my Foe!
I summon to man,
The Power of the Crow!

With Cosmic Energy!
And Radiant Might!
His Pendant emitted,
A Swirling Green Light!

There they stood,
Upon the floor,
A Defiant Formula!
The Definitive Four!

They unleashed their power,
To destroy Death's Door,
The Universal Power of...
The Forever Four!

Brimstone and chaos!
The hords! they came!
Evil whistled and shouted!
And called them by name!

On Lies! On Despair!
On Disease and Destruction!
On Torture and Chaos!

And Soul-Death Production!

Destroy one! Destroy two!
Destroy three and all!
I am He! I am He!
The Evil! That calls!

Chapter Eight

ENTER THE FOREVER FOUR:

I have the Look!
The 'Look of Lies!'
I Wield the Power!
Of a Dark Dark Smile!

Spice them both!
And what's the surprise?!
A **Dark Dark Angel**,
With Eternity's Eyes

The Eyes of Eternity,
Are something to see,
Look Up! Look Up!
At the Cosmic Sea!

The Unholy Grin!
The Unholy Grin!
I Release the Power!
The Power from Within!

Total Eclipse!
It did harness,
The Angel called the Realm!
...The Shade of Darkness!

The Shade of Darkness!
Evil cannot dwell,
Made of Matter,
That defeats Unholy Hell!

The Darkness that he called,
Was cold and eerie,
He transported them,
Into a Displacement Theory!

With the Eyes of Rapture!
And the Smile of More!
Quad-Energy Power!
Of The Forever Four!

Intrinsic Light!
With Flames of White!
A Human Star!
That Lit up the night!

Super Nova?
No! Super White!
He had the Power of,
Fantastic Light!

A Savior Star!
To Behold!
"I release the Light,

Of Forever Gold!"

Across the Realm,
Flew Johnny's Quest,
He incinerated demons,
With Flames that Blessed!

Battle Girl,
And the Staff that swirled,
She changed into,
A **Forever Girl**!

ChatterBox! ChatterBox!
A Girl of Light!
FlutterFly! FlutterFly!
Became FlutterFlight!

Charged with Energy,
And Radiant Light,
No longer a Battle,
A Forever Fight!

Forever Girl,
And the Girl of Light,
Meshed into one,
And this they did recite,

"Release Me Demon!
Release Me Right!
I attack you with,
FlutterFlight!

The Staff of Power,
I do Hurl!
I Release! I Release!
Forever Girl!!!!"

At the speed of Flutter!
At the speed of Flight!
The Staff flew faster
And into the night,

Burning it went!
Higher! Higher!
She called the Staff!
Jamaican SoulFire!

Rasta Fire!
Crucified Door!
Demons Forever!
Forever No More!

The Mind's Eye!
A Tornado to fly!
Up above!

He soared so High!

With the Sword of Sadness,
In His hand,
And the Power of God,
At His Command!

Poems of Power,
He did recite,
"Banish these Demons!
This Day! This Night!"

Evil's Demons,
Looked to the sky,
They did fear,
And they did cry,

They screamed! They panicked!
Danger! Danger!
Beware! Beware!
God's Resonating Chamber!

Clever recited his poems,
Up high,
And Heavenly Lightning,
Came from the sky,

Clever became,
God's Poetic Chamber!
Resonating! Resonating!
With Holy Danger!

The Sword of Sadness!
It did glow!
And Blasted Death's Doorman!
Through Unholy Door!

He called forth the power,
To Close and Heal!
The Power Obeyed!
And it did Seal!

Defeated Death's Doorman!
They evened the score,
The Holy Quad-Power of...
The Forever Four!

The Dog Tag Amulet,
Became a Green Swirl,
Intrinsic Light,
And Forever Girl,

It did swirl,
And change its angle,
And then was gone,

Was Dark Dark Angel,

Battle Boy,
The Mighty Lever,
He changed back to,
Clever! Clever!

Together and Forever,
They Heavenly Scored!
The Amazing Powers,
Of the Forever Four!

Together Their Powers!
They Heavenly Beamed!
The Holy Super Powers,
Of a Super Tag Team!

Alone! Again!
In a Hurricane Night,
Stood Clever! Clever! Clever!
In His Boots of Light!

As he pondered a thought,
How long would it last?
He knew he was the result,
Of an Inescapable Past!

A Golden Stone Road,
Appeared before his feet,
Clever to Destiny,
He had promised to keep,

Tears of Love,
Came to His Eyes,
Thoughts of his Family,
Friends, and their lies,

He knew it was time!
A Journey to Endeavor!
This Dark Mystical Warrior,
And the Brick of Forever!

The End

Clever! Clever!
&
The Book of Forever

"Hi!
My name is Clever! Clever!
And I live in the Book of Forever."

Once upon a time, in a land far, far away
a brave woman feared for the safety of
her baby son's life; his name was Clever.
After she placed her son in a basket, she
put the basket in the stream. The basket,
with baby Clever laying asleep in it,
floated down stream to a Powerful King's
Palace. The mighty king was called
Horarah. The Palace was like another land
rich with gold, people dressed in
extravagant-beautiful clothing, and the
gardens were breath-taking enchantments
of wonder.

Clever! Clever! Clever!
Was left in a house,
Tornado bum-rushed him,
And he couldn't get out,

Like a sardine can,
Riding the stars,
Like Dorothy and Toto,
In the Wizard of Oz,

Fear in his heart,
To make a last stand,
The house ended up,
In another land,

Drenched in blood,
And vacuumed packed,
Away from his mother,
He couldn't get back,

The house whirled around,
With such a kick,
That it crushed and smashed,
A big bad witch,

The folks of the village,
Cheered and grinned,
They ran like punks,
Because the witch had a twin,

Faith from the heavens,
Came to his side,
She came in a bubble,

A most vicious ride,

With the power of God!
She raised her hand!
She pointed to his feet,
In this distant land,

What do you think,
Was at hand?
That's right kids!
"Look Timberlands!"

From sneakers to Boots,
Like a saw to a chain,
Clever was ecstatic,
And this he proclaimed,

"The witch she tried me,
While I watched,
But all she got,
Was static shock!"

She stared at Faith,
And screamed for an hour,
Hands hurt and burned,
"The Boots have Power??!!!"

To Clever's amazement,
Now this was rare,
He looked at his boots,
"Hey! Home to Bellaire!"

Faith wished him luck,
As he ran from here,
Tears from her eyes,
As she disappeared,

Her tears hit the pavement,
With a brilliant light,
The stone went from old,
To yellow white,

Clever gazed upon,
An amazing trick,
Walking on a road,
Made of magic brick,

The Ten Commandments,
Were inscribed in gold,
She gave him a decree:
"Follow the Yellow Brick Road!"

With a puff of smoke,
Helen off to Troy,
The witch cried out,

"I'm going to get you boy!"

The witch made a vow,
To get those boots,
A promise to Clever,
She would shoot! shoot! shoot!

A cell in hand,
To call her goons,
An evil grin,
That flew on a broom,

Clever to the game,
He would be late!
The star quarterback,
But this was his fate!

A map in need,
To navigate the land,
Clever perplexed,
By the sign post stand,

"Which way do I Go?
Which way is best?
North? South? East?
Or West, West, West?"

He heard a strange voice,

On a distant pole,
Clothes stuffed with hay,
Made of precious gold,

"If you let me down,
I promise to decide,
Push down the nail,
And thus I will slide,"

He introduced himself,
With a quick little rhyme,
"Thank you for freedom,
From the Jaws of Time!"

Then in the road,
He did a silly dance,
This Whimsical Creature!
This Scarecrow Man!

The witch appeared,
A dreadful clone,
Trapped inside,
The bewitching zone,

Like Jeepers Creepers,
She could taste our fear!
She swooped down on us,
"Oh Dear! Oh Dear!"

His fist met her jaw,
He put her in check,
A scream from the witch,
"My neck! My neck!"

Clever screamed and yelled,
"It's time to go!"
As he watched his Brave friend,
Fight his Evil foe,

She rubbed her jaw,
Pissed and vexed,
Then she called forth,
A Deadly Hex!

"With the Eyes of Demons!
From the Pits that Smell,
Burn Crow Man! Burn!
Burn to Hell!"

Knowledge was the quest,
That he had followed,
He stammered, he ran,
And then he hollered!

"Fire! Fire! Fire!
Put it out!"
The witch and her broom,

On the old cottage house,

One on foot,
And one on skates,
They ran from the witch,
And her song of hate,

Like Speedy Gonzalez,
In the Mystic Land,
Here they encountered,
A Wood Chopping Man,

Clever baffled,
At this awesome sight,
The Scarecrow Man,
And this he did recite:

"There he stood,
This Silver Man!
A Metallic Mortal,
With an Iron Hand,

A Silver Power,
With a Silver Tan,
Spit/Polish with,
A Salute so Grand,

"With Aluminum Skin,

A Hero in a Book,
An Immortal Statue,
With an Eternal Look,

Look up in the Sky,
Its rain not Sand,
If you Count to Nine,
It's a Frozen Tin Man!"

Black Black Gold,
And Texas Tea,
Who would deliver,
It from the sea?

The Dynamic Duo,
Found a bucket of oil,
He who wins,
Takes all the spoils,

The Tin Can Man,
A Work of Art,
And all he wanted,
Was a Heart, Heart, Heart,

The two became three,
And so goes the story,
They walked along the brick,
The brick of glory,

So we turn the page,
To hidden spot,
Deep in the jungle,
Right down the block,

Terrified to death,
And holding hands,
That's when they met,
The Courageous Lion Man!

He growled and snarled,
Like nothing mattered,
That's when Clever shouted,
"Everyone scatter!"

He chased them here,
And he chased them that,
All he got,
Was a big old slap,

The lion cried out,
"You hit me on the nose!
Now I'm hurt,
And this I propose,"

He snorted, he sniggered,
And sniggered and snagged,
Then he cried out,

Like a big old fag,

He was unhappy,
And Alone,
They invited him to visit,
The Mystic Dome,

From out of the forest,
Searching for home,
Clever and the three,
Saw the Mystic Dome,

They ran across the fields,
They skipped and leaped,
The Woman of Darkness,
Put them fast asleep,

From the Heavens and Stars,
A Food of the Gods,
Unknown to Zeus,
And Unfound by Mars,

A delicious treat,
With the Scent of Banana,
The Fantastic Four,
Were Blessed with Manna!

The wizard be quested,

To make a wish,
Clever laid it out,
Like a big old fish,

He began to whine,
In the Majestic Dome,
"I'm tired of this place!
I want to go home!"

The Wizard knew,
This boy was wise,
So he stood and hid,
Behind his disguise,

I'll make you a promise,
But I won't shake your hand,
I will take you to,
This Promise Land,

Before I grant,
This favor in this room,
Bring me the Witch's,
Magic Broom!

Clever and his friends,
Were shocked and dismayed,
Contemplating about,
The deal he had made,

This would surely End,
End in Strife!
The witch will kill us,
And take our life!

The wizard raised his voice
"That's all for Now!"
Deliver Me the Broom,
Or Get Out of Town!"

The sky was filled,
With A Mighty Lever!
They all swooped down,
And grabbed Clever! Clever!

Dreaded monkeys!
With wings on their back!
"We demand you stop,
And bring Clever back!"

What just happened?
Now wait, wait, wait,
Throw Clever in,
The Room of Fate!

Across the room,
He did find,
The Hour Glass,

And the Sands of Time,

All this pressure,
Blowing his mind,
He heard the Witch,
And her Lyrical Rhymes,

Values and morals,
At an all time low,
Trapped on the island,
Of Monte Cristo,

Clever escaped,
From the Room of Fate,
And met his friends,
At the dark, dark gate,

Witch in her heels,
Ran really fast,
Troops in the car,
Forgot to get gas,

With soldiers around them,
The witch slammed the door,
Surrounded and trapped,
Was The Fantastic Four!

With the broom and soldiers,

To her side,
Games, toys, tricks,
And vicious lies,

"I'm gonna get you boy!"
"I'm gonna get you good!"
"Trespassing in,
In my neighborhood!"

She lunged at him,
And hit him hard,
Knocked Clever down,
Like a deck of cards,

She jumped on him,
And thus began to punch,
Made the Clever boy,
Throw up his lunch,

She hit him in the stomach,
And hit him up above,
That's when her troops cheered,
"The Witch Drew Blood!"

Down for the count,
He had felt her sting,
Jumping around him,
"The Demon Queen!"

Dancing around him,
Singing her song,
She recited from this!
Her Evil Tongue,

"Float like a Butterfly!
Sting like a Bee!
I am the best!
I can beat Ali!

Day by Day!
And Night by Night,
Everyone can see!
I'm the Winner of this Fight,

A Mistress of Destruction!
This Magic land!
No one can beat,
My Mighty Hand!

Like a Diamond to a Heart!
A Club to a Spade!
Your Power's Gone!
Now become My Slave!

If you make a Wrong Choice
Here tonight,
I promise to unleash,

My Angry Knife!"

Bruised and battered,
Battered and bruised,
Clever asked the question,
"How did I lose?"

His friends all around him,
Hot and mad,
Clever face down,
And she was glad,

A voice in his head,
Dizzy and bothered,
Then he remembered,
What faith had hollered,

"There's nothing you can't finish,
That you didn't start,
With confidence and knowledge,
In your heart,"

With the force of his friends,
In his soul,
This is Clever! Clever!
And the story he told,

Built like a Champion,

And built for Speed,
Determine to end,
This Demon's Siege,

Clever and his boots,
Began to glow,
His body went vertical,
Above the floor,

Floating in the air,
Like a Cross on Fire,
He looked at the witch,
And this he inspired:

"Eyes of Day,
And Vision of Night,
Let no Evil escape,
Escape my Sight,

Let all those who worship,
Evil's Might,
Beware Clever! Clever!
and His Boots of Light!"

He kicked her once
And he kicked her twice,
The witch got up,
And said "I'm all right!"

She shouted to her troops,
Her Troops of Hire,
"Hand Me The Broom!
The Broom of Fire!"

The Scarecrow Man,
upon his face,
He saw a vision,
he knew he would hate,

She lit him up,
With her dreadful lance,
We all watched in horror!
As he did his dance,

Clever quickly grabbed,
The Bucket of Power,
He would be the Hero!
The Man of the Hour!

But before he threw,
The Bucket of Woe,
The witch screamed in terror
"No! No! No! No!"

The witch staggered back,
As she began to fall,
Her Reign of Power,

In the Mighty Hall,

She tripped on fear,
This she would endeavor,
Defeated by a Man,
Named Clever! Clever! Clever!

With the Power of God!
With the power that followed,
The water tore her open,
And this she did holler:

I'm Melting! I'm Melting!
I'll tell you the truth,
Clever has defeated me!
In His Mighty Boots!

Clever to the chase,
He had empowered,
He conquered the witch,
And thus he would follow,

Clever gave the broom,
The Upper Hand!
Hurry up Man!
Get me out of this land!

The wizard astonished,

Total Disbelief,
He asked himself,
"How could she be beat?"

Said to himself
"Now I have the Power!"
I am the Wizard!
No! God of the Hour!"

Clever! Clever!
Tried to shake his Hand,
"Hold up a second! second!
Wait a minute! Man!"

"Make yourself at home,
While I take a shower,
I'll be a Minute,
No! I'll be an Hour!"

The Wizard a Hoax!
A Big Fat Slam,
Nothing more,
Than a Flim Flam Man!

He hid behind,
Some Big Old Drapes,
Plotting and Scheming,
Planning His Escape,

"Your flight will be quick!
Your flight will be soon!"
He pushed Clever! Clever!
From The Grand Balloon!

Clever told the Wizard,
"Don't leave me alone!
If you don't take me now,
I'll never get home!"

The Wizard laughed a smile,
And said "It's Too Late!
That's what you get
For depending on Fate!

The boy with his boots,
Said "I'm Stuck Forever!"
That's when a voice said,
"Clever! Clever! Clever!"

"You always had,
The Power to get Home,
You just had to believe,
In the Power of Your Own!"

Clever asked Faith,
"Will I see you again?"
"Not in the world,

Of the Promised Land,"

This was the last time,
They would see Clever,
His friends who walked,
The Brick of Forever,

"So with the Dog Tag Amulet,
Around his neck,
Power unleashed,
As he recited these text,

With the Power of Knowledge!
With the Power I Command!
Virtues of Life!
And Melanin Man!

My Dark Dark Sky!
A Vision that Looms!
I am the Master,
Of the Colorful Cards of Doom!

With the Sword of Sadness,
In My Hand!
Take Clever! Clever!
From this Mystic Land!

The crystalline matter in his boots began to glow, and a brilliant burst of colorful radiant energy began whirling through the air a-round Clever. His friends had to backup to a safe distance, or they would be swept away by its awesome fury. As Clever! Clever! vanished into thin air, he waved goodbye to his Wonderful and Amazing Friends - the Scarecrow, Tin Can Man, Courageous Lion, and Faith.

Clever vanished in a brilliant storm of color-ful light. His friends could only hear his Poem of Remem-brance...

"I finally understand that as I grow smaller and smaller in my universe, equal to the size of a grain of salt,
that I will not cease to exist, but in a factual yet un-seemly reality, I am becoming one with the universe."

And with understanding his destiny, Clever! Clever! smiled and was at peace with himself.

"I finally understand that I am Me...

... I am The Hero of Antiquity!"

The End

Clever! Clever!
&
The Land of Whatever

"Hi!
My name is Clever! Clever!
And I got lost in the Land of Whatever.
And here we go…"

Clever! Clever! Clever!
Fell down a hole,
A downward spiral,
As time did unfold,

Matter all around him,
Folded and displaced,
Alternate dimensions,
Of time and space,

Woken from his dream,
Things were not simple,
Clever had experienced,
A "Time-Differential,"

What is this place,
He had endeavored?
Unknown to Clever,

Was the Land of Whatever!

He felt an unbalance,
In time and space,
He knew it was "Time,"
Time to escape!

With a Dog Tag Amulet,
In his hand,
Power unleashed,
As he recited his plan:

"With the Power of Knowledge!
With the Power I Command!
Virtues of Life,
And Melanin Man!

My Dark Dark Sky,
A Vision that Looms!
I am the Master,
Of the Colorful Cards of Doom!

With 'The Sword of Sadness'
In my hand,
Propel Clever! Clever!
Through this Unnatural Land!"

Warping Time, Time,

Matter and Space,
Clever disappeared,
Through a Three Dimensional Gate,

With Quantum Mechanics,
A Power and Source,
I am The Master,
Of Destiny's Course!

As he dimensionally-shifted,
High and low,
Clever and his Boots,
Began to glow,

What just happened?!
Now wait, wait, wait!
I'm falling! I'm falling!
And now it's too late!

He hit the ground,
With the force of a star,
And made a crater,
The size of Mars,

He pondered a thought,
"How long would it last?"
He was the result,
Of an Inescapable Past!

Was Clever going crazy?
Had the boy lost his mind?
Under the tree,
He did find!

Clever! Clever!
"Up in the tree!"
Did you see,
Or was it just me?

Did he see a Cat?
A Cat with a Smile?
No! a Dark Angel,
With Eternity's Eyes,

"Hold up a minute!
Now don't just go!
I want to ask a Quick
"Quick Pro Quo!"

Riddle me with Kindness,
Or Riddle me Hate,
Why does He sit,
On the Tall, Tall Gate?

Empowered by Kindness!
Rejecting Hate!
Answer the question,

before it's too late!

An Elliptical Orbit,
A Man of Egg!
A big round body,
With short little legs!

Doesn't He know,
He can't cheat Fate?
The Round, Round Man,
On the Tall, Tall Gate!

THE QUEEN OF CARDS

Clever went in,
"The Quiet Quiet Hall,"
A wonderful gala,
The size of a mall!

He looked up,
And what did he see,
A colorful flat card,
The size of a tree,

Black, Black Gold,
And Texas Tea,
Who would deliver it,

From the sea?

She introduced herself,
With a Trick or Treat,
Kneel before me! Kneel!
And kiss my feet!

I am the Queen,
The Queen of The Cards!
Talk to me about,
The Heaven and Stars!

She sat on her throne,
And this she did boast,
You are my Guest,
And I am your Host,

Obey My Instructions,
Or walk like the Dead,
Off! Off! Off!
Off! Off with His Head!

Clever to himself,
This was erratic,
He had encountered,
A Female Fanatic!

In Her hand!

It did Sing!
A Dark Scorpion,
With a Deadly Sting!

A Blood Thirsty Queen,
With a Crazy Fling,
Be My Lover,
Or be My King,

Thought she was finished,
Thought she was close,
She kept on Rhyming,
With her Lyrical Jokes,

I am the Queen,
The Most! Most! Most!
I am the Bacon,
The Honey and the Toast!

Clever told himself,
Escape from here!
This Lady's crazy,
And thus I Fear!

The Scorpion Sang,
A Sonic Cheer!
Made Clever Clever,
Put his hands to his ears!

A Mistress of Destruction!
This Magic land!
No one can beat,
My Mighty Hand!

A Diamond to a Heart!
A Club to a Spade!
Beat Me at My Game,
Or become My Slave!

Clever couldn't start!
He couldn't finish!
Out of the shadows,
A Venomist Sentence!

Clever gazed upon,
A vicious feat,
Unlike the Witch,
She was known to cheat,

From out of Hell!
Couldn't find Dennis!
She played her Card,
The Card of Menace!

It didn't come for Venus,
And didn't play Tennis!
Appeared from the Darkness,

Was "The Evil Violinist!"

"I'll play you a tune!
A tune of Gold!
But before too long,
I'll have your Soul!"

The Scorpion sang,
"The Song of Sam!"
The Queen called forth,
Her Deadly Lamb!

As Clever! Clever! Clever!
Was turning around,
He encountered an Evil,
"An Evil Clown!

"I am The Card!
The Card of Hate!
I have been known,
To smile at Fate!

With the taste of Sugar,
With flavor of a Shake,
I dance to the tune,
Of "Carrot Carrot Cake!"

From across the room,

On Her Evil Throne,
Clever knew,
He was trapped and alone,

He looked at Heaven,
And up at the Stars,
Then he called forth,
The Power of God!

With the Power of God,
He raised his hand!
"I Have The Power!
The Power of Man!

With the 'Card of Q,'
At My Command!
With 'The Sword of Sadness,'
In My Hand!

My Dark Dark Sky!
A Vision that Looms!
I am the Master of,
The Colorful Cards of Doom!

Faster than faster,
Than the Speed of Light,
Using Quantum,
Theory as I write!

Here I stand,
This "Melanin Man,"
Absorbing the Spectrum,
From a Cosmic Land!

My Mind enhanced,
For a Genetic Fight,
My Soul a Conduit,
Of Ambient Light!

Alternate worlds,
My thoughts and me,
A smile, smile, smile,
Up there in a tree!

Knowledge of the Universe,
Roam my mind,
Transforming Matter,
Essence, and Time!

To the top of Wonderland!
Top of Oz!
My Eyes a Beacon,
Of the Stars!

So faster than faster,
Than the Speed of Light!
Can you feel My Power?

Can you feel My Might?

With a Dog Tag Amulet,
And a Golden Tap,
With the Power of Fripp!
And the Power of Frapp!"

Power Punching them,
To the floor,
He was the Victor!
This Battle Boy!

With power endowed,
He evened the score,
And thus defeated,
Was "The Ugly Four!"

The Cards did wither,
They did fall,
They fell in defeat,
In the Quiet Hall,

JACK RABBIT AND CRAFTY CLOCK

Didn't have a nickel,
And didn't have a dime,
Out the door,
He did find!

Down the road,
And near a sign,
Pouring a hot drink,
For The Father of Time,

There they sat,
On a rock,
An Old Jack Rabbit,
And Crafty Clock,

He wasn't Bugs,
And he wasn't funny,
They sat and ate,
Some jam and some honey,

Black, Black Gold,
And Texas Tea,
Clever! Clever!
Who may you be?

They drank, drank, drank,
And this they did hearty,
Had Clever Boy crashed,
The Boston Tea Party?

I 'm Clever! Clever!
Clever as ever!
I have the knowledge,

Of the stars and the weather,

The Rabbit gave a smirk,
He gave an evil stare,
He knew, Clever knew,
He was the Hare!

Like the Silly Rabbit,
On a Box of Trix,
Taunted Clever Clever,
"Riddle Me This!"

"I am the Minute!
I am the Hour!
I am the Birds,
The Bees, and the Flower!

Do you have a flower?
Do you have a dime?
Please, Please Sir,
Tell me the Time!"

I'm late, late, late!
And this I do hate!
I'm late, late, late!
With Time and Fate!

He's going to be unhappy,

He's going to be sad,
He's going to be really,
Really mad!

He's going to be mad,
This I hate,
The man who lives,
At the Dark, Dark Gate!

Clever did ponder,
And he did think,
He knew "Old Jack,"
Was the Missing Link!

Clever didn't argue,
Cuss or fight,
Looked at the Rabbit,
And this he did recite,

"You there, You there!
Drinking the tea,
You are the Answer!
You are the Key!

"You are Time!
Time and Space!
You are The Answer,
To The Dark, Dark Gate!

The Jack Rabbit! Astonished!
Total Disbelief!
He looked at the boy's,
Unfair Defeat!

"The boy solved The Puzzle!
The Riddle of Time!"
Drove the Jack Rabbit,
Right out of his mind!

You won't get me boy!
I'll tell you true,
You won't read the book!
"The Taming of the Shrew!"

With a puff of smoke,
Crafty Clock was gone!
Clever to himself,
"It was a Con!"

Clever tried to catch,
Where Gravity Dwells,
The Rabbit took off,
Like a Bat out of Hell!

I can't be late,
And I can't be loose,
I have a date,

With Old Mother Goose!

Like the Road Runner running,
Running a Race,
The Rabbit distorted Time!
Time and Space!

Catch Me! Catch Me!
If you can!
I am the Exit!
The Sign Post Stand!

Catch Me! Catch Me!
If you can!
The Doorway! The Doorway!
To Whatever Land!

I 'm in a hurry,
To get things done,
I rush and rush,
Till life's no fun,

I wish I Could!
Fly, fly, fly,
I'm in a hurry,
And don't know why,

I don't know why,

I run so fast!
I never give out,
Give out of gas!

My Shoes! My Shoes!
They're not new!
Zero to sixty,
In five-point two!

My Watch! My Watch!
I'm running out of time!
I'm leaving Clever Clever,
Far behind!

I'd better, better,
Pick up my pace!
There's no room,
For second place!

So here I go!
Boom! Boom! Boom!
Bye Clever Clever!
Zoom! Zoom! Zoom!

The Rabbit beaten,
By a Genius of Art,
Thought to himself,
He was smart, smart, smart,

The three became two,
And the story unfolds,
Clever chased Jack,
Down Forbidden Road!

He didn't find Jill,
And he didn't find Jack,
The Rabbit was gone,
And that was a fact!

CATERPILLAR MAN

He heard a strange voice,
On a distant mold,
Sitting on a Room,
A Room of Gold,

Up to Heaven,
With Ulysses' Bow!
Down to Hell,
With a Halo!

So Up to Heaven,
And Down to Hell,
What is that scent?
What is that smell?

Clever spun around,

With an electric fan,
In Total Disbelief!
A Caterpillar Man!

Look up in the sky,
As matter of fact,
It's a Bird! It's a Bird!
No! A Big Fat Rat!

On top of the Mush Room!
He did find,
A Caterpillar Man,
With an Elusive Rhyme!

You are the Reason!
You are the Rhyme!
The Boy! The Boy!
Of Definitive Time!

You are the one,
Who does not toddle,
You are the Boy!
The Genius In A Bottle!

Riddle me with Reason,
Riddle me with led,
A Caterpillar Man,
With a thousand little legs!

A corn cob pipe,
And a big little nose,
A long, long torso,
With pink little toes!

The smoke filled his head,
Dizzy and bothered,
He obeyed Pillar-Man,
He screamed and hollered,

He hypnotized Clever,
The Big Long Stack,
Then he danced, danced,
The "Cabbage Patch!"

You have a choice!
See my dilemma?
Run tell others,
But don't tell Linda!

Will you take a fork?
Will you take a knife?
Will you take a piece,
From the left or right?

I have a plan,
Which doesn't include you,
Here! Take a bite!

Chew! Chew! Chew!

Eat right up,
At the Heaven and Stars!
The Heavens! The Heavens!
Unfound by Mars!

Clever ate a piece,
Of the Room of Power,
Then he grew tall,
As a Water Tower!

Caterpillar Man said,
Try and adore!
Then grow small,
Till you touch the floor!

Clever fell down,
Down to the floor!
All he could see,
Was a Vertigo!

Fire! Fire! Fire!
Burning in My Heart,
Shouldn't have swallowed,
Why did I start?

Body laid straight,

Like a flat, flat loaf,
Clever was down,
And out of hope,

Why did I eat,
"The Food of the Gods?!!"
Now, I can't see,
The Heaven and the Stars,

A map in need,
To navigate the land,
Clever perplexed,
By the Sign Post Stand!

"Which way is up?
Which way is best?
North? South? East?
Or West, West, West?

Caterpillar Man said,
You're in a bind,
Can you now see,
Why Justice is Blind?

Smoking his pipe,
The Pipe of Hate!
Clever had to stop Him!
Before it's too late!

With the Power of God,
To stop his Foe,
Clever screamed and yelled,
No! No! No!

In his heart,
He did find,
The Power of a Peace!
A Biblical Rhyme!

Losing his Vision,
But not His Dream,
Now he plays,
As Ray Charles sings,

With the Knowledge of Eternity!
With the Stare of her Eyes!
I now know where,
Where Destiny Lies!

Lightning and Thunder,
In His Eyes!
Power Unleashed,
In The Dark Dark Sky!

Clever and His Boots,
Began to Glow!
His body went vertical,

Above the floor!

Floating in the air,
Like a Cross on Fire,
Clever felt a burn,
The Burn of Higher!

I am Clever! Clever! Clever!
Clever I Am!
WHERE ARE YOU?!
CATERPILLAR MAN!

I'm Clever! Clever! Clever!
I'm Strong as ever!
I have the Power!
I have "The Lever!"

I will Not Obey You!
Now or Later!
I Cry for Marcus!
The Roman Gladiator!

Power Unleashed,
Where I Stand!
WHERE ARE YOU??!!!!
CATERPILLER MAN!!!!!!!

In "The Room of Mush,"

He did zoom,
Hidden inside,
Was a Glass-Cocoon!

The Caterpillar Man,
Found his Room of Gold,
An Incubating Chamber!
A McCullan's Gold!

The Glass-Cocoon,
A Hidden Blender!
A Metamorphic Chamber,
With a Deadly Agenda!

In the Glass-Cocoon,
He did find!
The Wings of Freedom,
And The Jaws of Time!

He grew long teeth!
Sharp as a saw!
His pink little feet!
Turned "Killer Claw!"

He did CHANGE!
He did MORPH!
No longer a worm,
"A KILLER MOTH!"

Busting out of,
"The Room of Goo!"
He shouted to Clever,
I COME FOR YOU!!!

Clever reflected!
A Vision it seems,
A Hero down on love!
And out of hope and dreams!

My Dark Dark Sky,
A Vision that Looms!
I am the Master,
Of the Colorful Cards of Doom!

With Love and Justice,
In his Heart,
Clever did battle,
With Killer Moth!

With The Power of Dark!
With The Power of Love!
He called forth a force,
From "High Up Above!"

With the Sword of Sadness,
In His Hand,
His Presence was felt,

In The Unnatural Land!

So up above,
He stood so high,
This Dark Dark Man,
In a Dark Dark Sky!

With the Love of God,
He did inspire,
He lit up the heavens,
Like a "Phoenix of Fire!"

In the Mist,
Of a Mystical Hurricane Night,
A Marvel! A Wonder!
An Omnipotent Sight!

Look! Look! Look!
Up in the sky!
He's Clever! Clever! Clever!
That Super Guy!

"I am the Star!
I am the Power!
I am the Hero!
God of the Hour!

Wisdom and Knowledge,

At an all time High,
He knocked Killer Moth,
Out of the sky,

The Cosmic Force!
Tore Killer's Flesh!
He fell to the ground,
In a Burned-Green Mess!

In a quick, quick flash!
Clever did zoom!
Over his foe!
He did loom!

"With the Sword of Sadness,
In My Hand!
With the Power of Knowledge,
At My Command!

I Command the Heavens,
And The Holy Cloth!
Destroy! Destroy!
This Killer Moth!"

Light from the Heavens,
Came to his sword!
Thus defeated,
Was the Killer Moth!

With Holy Energy,
And Radiant Light,
Clever! Clever! Clever!
Took Caterpillar's Life!

When the dust had cleared,
And the smoke was gone,
Clever found himself,
All alone!

With the Will to Live,
And the Power to Die,
Take me through,
My Dark Dark Sky!

THE RABBIT AND THE MAD HATTER

What did the horror,
Of my eyes did it matter!
The Rabbit drinking tea,
With a Drunken Mad Hatter!

"You There! You There!
Drinking the tea!
You are The Answer!
You are the Key...

...Circle, Circle,

In the sky,
Around I go,
And spit in your eye,

Circle, Circle,
In My Hare,
You can't move,
And I don't care,

Zero to a million,
In five point flat,
I have you now!
Rabbit named Jack!

At Super-Speed,
You're sure to leave!
"Imprison Jack!
JumpDrive Speed!"

Lightning and thunder,
In the sky!
Imprisoned forever!
Way up high!

Trapped in a Tornado!
Suspended in Air!
He couldn't move!
This Abominable-Hare!

Couldn't get comfortable,
And all alone,
Trapped inside,
A Containment Dome!

From a Bunny to Rabbit,
Like a Jekyll to a Hyde!
Old Jack Rabbit,
Went Stalk Crazy-Wild!

Not a box of cereal,
With a Hidden Quiz!
No Silly Rabbit!
Trix are for Kids!

Jack Caught Off-guard!
And Perplexed!
Caught inside!
"A Clever Vortex!!!!!"

Let me introduce,
This next, next matter!
I am known as,
"The Drunken Mad Hatter!

I am Mr. Nasty!
Nasty Dang Nabbit!
You won't do to me,

How you did Jack Rabbit!

I am the Big!
The Big, Big Sleaze!
I am the Bacon,
The Honey, and the Cheese!

Lizard and Rodents!
Rodents and Rats!
What can you tell me,
About that, that, that?

Don't under-estimate,
Man and his Hat!
I have the power!
The Power to attack!

Pay attention please!
Clever if you can?
The eye is, is!
Quicker than the hand!

Don't get me wrong,
What I pull out this Hat!
A preconceived notion,
Of Magic and Jack!

You best be sure,

What I pull out this hat!
It won't be a Bunny,
And it won't be Jack!

What do we have?
Two little "T's,"
Come to life,
And do my deed!

I have two little T's,
In my hand!
Crush them up,
And throw them in the sand!

A little sunlight,
Is all they need!
Up from the ground,
Sprang my "Dragon Seeds!"

Too Much Sin!
Too Much Sin!
How Are You Doing?!!!
How Have You Been?!!!

Night by Night!
Sin by Sin!
We are the two!
The Looking-Glass Twins!

I am fast!
And I am slow,
I am McPhee!
And I am McPhoe!

You don't want to fight us!
You don't want to tangle,
We are the Notorious,
Dobblegangers!

We are Special!
A Special Gift!
We can Multiple,
And Dimensionally-shift!

All that talk,
Getting Clever down,
He looked at them,
With his face to the ground,

Things were getting,
Way out of hand,
For the Genius, Genius,
Genius Man,

In his heart,
Clever did find,
The Power to stop,

Their Mad, Mad Rhyme,

Clever called The Power!
The Power of Time,
The Power replicated him,
A trillion times!

He Dimensionally-shifted,
A million and two,
And hit them hard,
With the old one-two!

THE MAN AT THE DARK, DARK GATE

What just happened?
Now Wait! Wait! Wait!
Who stands watch,
At the Dark, Dark Gate?

Who is this man?
The gate he keeps,
And why does he walk,
An "Endless Sleep?"

And then I saw him!
In the Shadows of Fate!
The Man at the Dark,
Dark Dark Gate,

A Mystic Anomaly!
A Warrior of Fate!
Stand aside,
Shadow of Fate!

From out of the darkness,
His eyes pierced my soul,
Eyes of flame,
And his stare so cold,

From the crack of his mouth,
He showed a dark grin,
His voice shook my bones,
Like a horrible sin,

I am your Momma!
I am your Daddy!
I am the Shadow,
That's in the Ally!

I am the One!
The Beaver! The Beaver!
The One! The One!
The Master Dream Weaver!

You want to leave,
The Land of Whatever!
I can't permit it!

Never! Never!

Out of the shadows,
In this hidden land,
Appearing before me!
A Jabberwock-Man!

Riddle me this!
Riddle me that!
I see you took care of,
The man with the Hat!

Once upon a life time,
Long, long ago,
When times were simple,
And life was slow,

Peanut Butter Toast!
Toasted Ham!
This is a Tale,
Of "Sam I Am!"

Dusted Off!
The Death of A Nation!
Thus to reveal,
A "Sick Revelation!"

The Book of Peace,

A Hidden Agenda!
It lied to them,
And it didn't tell Linda!

Apache to Cherokee!
Seminole to Soo!
Introduce our Nation,
...to Uncle Who?

Georgie Porgie,
Pudding Pie!
Invaded our land,
And thus would die!

Told by their lawyers,
Who were on vacation,
Tricked and defeated,
By an Alien Nation!

The Miccosoukee screamed,
What do I do?
Invaded our people,
And enslaved you!

Forget thee not!
The Trail of Tears!
My! My! My!
Oh Dear! Oh Dear!

The Civil War!
A War to endeavor,
A Break Down of Power!
And Oh Whatever??!!

Humpty Dumpty,
A Sherlock Sleuth,
Soldiers and Horses,
Didn't have a clue!

Slithy! Slithy!
Slithy and Slime!
Do you have the answer?
Can you break my rhyme?

Snick-Snack, Snick-Snack!
With a cat!
Snick-Snack, Snick-Snack!
Pattywack!

I want to leave,
This Looking-Glass Land,
You don't have to help me,
Or give me a hand,

Whatever Land,
Is one Big Show!
The answer to your question,

Is Portmanteau!

Out of the portal,
He did zoom,
He flew like the Cow,
Jumping over the moon.

Clever left Jabber-Man,
Standing alone,
"See you later man,
I'm going home."

The End

SPECIAL BONUS EDITION

Ray Charles: A Musical Daredevil
Dedicated to Ray Charles

He acquired all his powers,
In an incident!
Biochemical Hazard,
And thus it was sent!

A Musical Daredevil,
In our yard,
You know! You heard!
They call him Ray Charles!

"A Master of Darkness!
A Musician of Sound!
His music is Gospel!
Innovatively Profound!"

Out of Hell's Kitchen,
Spurred His Gift,
A Super-Human Hero,
From an unnatural myth!

A Tragic Hero,

With a Rhythmic Touch!
A Piano-Playing Man!
God gave him to Us!

Punished by Fate!
And his Tragic Past,
Destiny shaped Him!
A Legend of Jazz!

A Ghost of His Past,
Was all in the deal,
Memories of his Brother!
His Achilles Heel!

A Super Blind Man,
With Amazing Powers!
He would be the Hero!
The Star of the Hour!

Unbroken Love!
A Dream to Endeavor,
This Musical Marvel!
A Man like no other,

His Mother! A Promise!
He would keep,
Walking the World,
In "An Endless Sleep!"

Self-Esteem,
At an all time low,
He would be their Villain!
Their Musical Foe!

Sound and Touch!
Power was "The Lever!"
Marvel At This!
At A Black Man's Endeavor!

Power unleashed!
As "His Fingers Played the Keys!"
He brought Racism down,
To Its Weak Little Knees!

A Melanin Man!
Heightened Sensory Perceptions!
He foiled Georgia's Plan!
Her Great Deception!

An Unspeakable Evil!
Georgia's Tongue!
He conquered her,
And sang His Mighty Song!

The State tried to bind Him,
With restrictions and fines,
Now the whole Country sings,
"Georgia On My Mind."

Up to Heaven & Down to Hell

Up to Heaven and Down to Hell is a poetic track. The writings deal with inner soul searching discoveries and universal simplicities. Inspirations of poetic love, symbolism, and irony are expressed.

Just as country music tells us stories, Up to Heaven and Down to Hell does the same thing with heroes of old, present, and new ...defiant until the end. Poetic peace and lyrical justice is written from a Black Ideology.

Will you be able to withstand the mind-blowing turbulence of calm harmonic love while being swept away by lyrical rap? Each totally different, yet respectful of the other.

CASTAWAYS

So we turn the page,
To a hidden spot!
Deep dark Africa,
Right down the block!

The Trojan horse,
With a deadly gift!
Like the blond hair lady,
Launched a thousand ships!

Seeded in evil!
Like a spawn from hell!
"We come in peace!"
Was what they yelled,

Like Independence Day,
A predetermined fate,
They found our house!
They found the place!

A plan? A plot?
A hidden scheme!
Unpleasant! Distasteful!
A most fiendish scene!

Like a black hole,

Where gravity dwells!
Like a spider to a fly!
Like a bat in hell!

So away they sailed,
To a distant beach,
Singing their song,
"Shackles on my Feet!"

Like a sardine can,
Riding the stars,
Like Dorothy and Toto,
In the Wizard of Oz,

Drenched in blood,
And vacuumed packed!
Stolen from their mother!
They couldn't go back!

On a foreign shore,
Here they stand,
Old Saint Nick,
And Uncle Sam!

So ashes to ashes,
And dust to dust,
These trilogies are stories,
From you to us!

THE GRIM REAPER & SAM

I am SLAVERY!
Slavery I am!
Do you like,
The Grim Reaper and Sam?

I do not like,
This slavery I am,
I do not like,
The Grim Reaper and Sam,

Will you labor,
Labor for free?
Or will you labor,
Labor for me?

Leave me be,
Slavery I am!
I do not like,
The Grim Reaper and Sam!

I will not labor,
Labor for free!
And I will not labor,
Now don't you see?

Will you labor,

In the sun?
Or will you labor,
In front of a gun?

I will not labor,
In the sun!
I will not labor,
In front of a gun!

I will not labor,
Labor for free!
Nor will I labor!
Now don't you see?!

I do not like,
The Grim Reaper and Sam,
I do not like them,
Slavery I am.

THE HERO OF ANTIQUITY

With a heightened sense of discernment;
shaped and molded by an environment
and society that has en-gulfed and
entrapped me. Unable to command the
cosmic forces of my universe, here I
stand! A Ga-lactus! Snared and bound by
man's rule which feeds on the very core
that sustains life, my eternal spirit. Like a
butterfly that transcends its earthly
bounds, I too thirst. Yet sealed into a
cocoon that is glass-fashioned into a cast
system is my fate. A man voyaging
through time itself - searching for the
answer to his question. A sentient being
endowed with super ability, but stripped
of the catalyst to unleash cosmic power.
Am I the inescapable result of trilogies
long ago? But what if I am me? A Hero of
Antiquity!

THE COLORFUL CARDS OF DOOM

Sarcastically unappreciated self worth!
Unable to connect the dots of life! Alive!
All knowing! All powerful! A showman of
the "Glass-Class," A come-dian on stage
performing life's infinite role for truth.
Yet the mood swings do come, and again
anger and frustration are my closes
friends. At Destiny's table! Fate has dealt
its decisive hand, and I am the "Master-
Actor" imprinted and embossed on the
Colorful Cards of Doom!

MELANIN MAN

Faster than faster,
Than the speed of light!
Using quantum theory,
As I write!

Here I stand,
This "Melanin Man,
Absorbing the spectrum,
From a cosmic land,

My mind enhanced,
For a genetic fight,
My soul a conduit,
Of ambient light!

Alternate worlds,
My thoughts and me,
A smile, a smile,
Up there in a tree,

Knowledge of the universe,
Roams my mind,
Transforming matter,
Essence, and time,

To the top of wonderland!
To the top of OZ!
My eyes a beacon,
Of the stars,

So faster than faster,
Than the speed of light!
Can you feel my power?
Can you feel my might?

MY ELEMENTAL WOMAN

My Lady, I am pleading with you to
release me from the universal forces of
your love...Earth, Wind, Fire, and Soul!
Your Presence is the EARTH ... it
commands me to kneel and bow as an
African Prince would bow out of respect
for his Ebony Princess, as she sits
proudly on her African Throne.

Your Conversation is the WIND...pleasing,
yet distin-guished, intelligent, leaves me
wanting more!

Your Personality - like FIRE! POWERFUL,
EXPRESSIVE, SASSY, YET EMINATING
MAGNETIC WAVES OF LOVE IN ITS
PUREST FORM,

Your Voice is SOUL...a sweet sexy jazz
melody lightly stirred in a smooth rosy
wine; pleasing to the senses- Insatiable for
you!

Your Hair...a symbol of culture, pride,
identity, know-ledge, power and universal
truth,

Your Laughter...a comforting sound of joy
– Friend-ship,

Your Eyes..oh yes! Those two lovely rose
petals with delicate drops of water
sprinkled gently upon.

Loves Calling You sweetheart, please
answer...

UNIVERSAL RULES OF SCRABBLE

FOR 2 PLAYERS ONLY

CONTENTS
Thinking about you
Cannot sleep at night
Longing to hold you

SETUP
One must be patient for a seedling to grow
through the warm earth and stretch its
blossoms toward the life giving rays of the
sun. To look upon those rose petals as
they sparkle from the fertile water
nestled in the center of a rose is a
beautiful sight to behold.

Through nature's watchful eyes, this life-cycle takes persistence and nurturing.

<u>SCORING</u>
For your heart to blossom for me, I too must be pa-tient, persistent and nurture the fragrant petals of friendship, trust, respect, understanding, comfort, compassion, certainty, openness, kindness, sureness, reverence, and oh yes love.

<u>HOW TO WIN</u>
Like a mariner lost at sea uses the heavenly lights to navigate safely home, I too need your heavenly light to help me carefully navigate, meticulously steer and ever so gently nurture the twelve fragrant rose seedlings of your heart to blossom for me.

EXAMPLES OF WORD FORMATION AND SCORING

...Earth, Wind, Fire, and Soul!

Loves calling you sweetheart, please answer.

LOST HORIZON

Oh my love, I have searched,
And searched the world over,

I have searched deep in my soul,
Looking for that Lost Horizon,

But now my love,
I have found you in my heart,
Fore you are my beloved...Shangri-La!

IN SEARCH OF

Where is your love?
Where is your love?

Do I cross a secret horizon,
to find it in the Lost City of Shangri-La!
Or journey to the center of the earth,
to discover a golden key?

Where is your love?
Where is your love?
My Elemental Woman,
Must I possess a cosmic cube,
Of earth, wind, fire, and soul to find it?

Is it secretly hiding,
Under the cover like a puppy dog?
And you say,
"Stay under there,
Because you broke a lot of things,
The last time you came out."

Or is it held carefully like a butterfly,
In the palms of your hands,
Patiently waiting for me to energize,
It with the ebbing tide of my love?

SWEET NOVEMBER

Oh my love!
You wake up in the morning,
And you hear the mockingbirds,
Singing outside your windowpane,

You see the butterflies,
Gliding free in the clear morning sky,
Oh my love! I love December,
But you...you're my Sweet November.

WONDERFUL THINGS

I wonder about,
The things you say,
I wonder if,
You're going to stay,

I wonder about,
The things you do,
I'm curious,
I wonder about you.

From the first time,
I met you,
I asked myself,
"Who is this wonderful woman?"
So to you Wonder Woman...

The things you say,
And the things you do,
I wonder about,
The beautiful things within you.

Echoes from the heart.

WHO GOT PLAYED

Jack and Jill,
Went up the hill,
Respect me Jack,
Cause I'm on the pill!

Sweet little Dorothy,
In the Land of Oz,
The witch tired to kill her,
Without a cause!

Little Red,
And the big bad fox,
Had a dilemma,
In that little house,

Jack and the Giant,
Had a little fight,
Giant tried to kill him,
With an angry knife!

Ba Ba Black Sheep
Did all he could,
All he got,
Was three bags full!

The little old lady,

Living in a shoe,
A lot of kids,
What do I do?

Hanzel and Gretel,
With their greedy plot,
Almost ended up,
In the witch's pot.

THE SWORD OF SADNESS

The Sword of Sadness,
Pierced my Dark Soul!

It yelled and screamed,
An insane anger,
As clever Odysseus,
Lamented to the sirens,

The Sword of Sadness,
Pierced my Dark Soul!

Its double-twin blades of deceit,
Sealed the fate of mighty Achilles,
A condemned path of destruction,
Immortalized by man and treasured,
By the wet kiss of time,

The Sword of Sadness' mirrored
reflection,
Healed the Ancient Warrior's wound,
As its arrow shattered my heart,
Its cold shaft unsheathed,
To reveal terror,
To the core,
Of my pure essence,

The Sword of Sadness,
Sliced the brilliant light,
Of my Dark Soul!

Liquid pain flowed,
From the infliction,
And Happiness,
Did cry in despair,

The Sword of Sadness,
Did this!
And to It I say...
No More!

MY DARK SKY

Alone! In the mist,
Of a mystical hurricane night,
I watch the star-candle give birth,
To silhouette smiles,

In my Dark Sky,
They beckon toward a candle-lit sun,
That dangles like a spider,
Dancing on a single silk-spun thread,
On the verge of discovering the vastness,
Of the universe and its event horizon,

Me, myself, and I,
Alone... beneath My Dark Sky!

PRIORITY OR PREFERENCE

Priority or Preference?
Which one dwells in the collection?
Which one applies to this hypothetical
selection?

Arriving to work on time?
Is this a matter of Priority or Preference?

If you choose,
Priority over Preference,
Your job will survive,
Be it Preference however,
Your pay is docked at five,

Priority or Preference?
Which one dwells in the collection?
Which one applies,
To this hypothetical selection?

A banquet, a dance, a fashion show,
We tease,
Where is the coordinator?
Constructive criticism please,

What is this stigma of time?
Is it "Communal Potential Time?"

I will continue on,
With expedient haste,
This poem of play on words,
And timely mistake,

Priority or Preference?
Which one dwells in the collection?
Which one applies,
To this hypothetical selection?

"C' is for the spectrum,
That classifies men,
"P" is for the pigment,
Of our skin,

"T" is the third letter,
No more,
No less,
Now, can your answer,
Pass my test?

I am the sphinx!
I have given the clue!
Now, what is the answer,
To our "Socio-psychic Taboo?"

QUIETISM OR CONFORMITY

Quietism or Conformity?
Which will you choose?
I'm curious to know,
So please make your move,

This two-categorical system,
Arranged in a hierarchy,
Is not this the same,
As Trans-generational Suffering?

Quietism or Conformity?

Answer the question!
Or would you like to sit through,
Captain Kirk's "No Win Scenario?"

Quietism or Conformity?
Nzinga did not groan,
Instead, she sat proudly,
On her African throne,

You should remember me by now,
Because I taught you a lesson,
Or have you forgotten me by now,
The author of Priority or Preference.

THE NIGHT BEFORE SLAVERY

It was the night before slavery,
Ships in the sea,
Not one, not two,
Not even three,

Africa in peace,
And I in my cap,
Had just settled down,
For a long tropic nap,

When out in the village,
There rose such a clatter,
I sprang from my bed,
Like a drunken Mad Hatter,

Away to the forest,
To escape death and disaster,
I ran! I ran!
But this did not matter,

But what did the horror,
Of my eyes did appear?
Men with chains,
Carrying deadly gear!

My little old village,

Being pillaged and plundered,
My ears filled with terror,
From the smoke and the thunder!

More rapid than vultures,
The courses they came,
They killed and tortured,
And even changed our names!

On lies! On despair!
On death and destruction!
On torture and branding!
And slavery production!

To the west coast with one!
To the west coast don't fall!
Now fast away! Fast away!
Fast away all!

As fish swim around,
In the dark ocean deep,
They meet with the creatures,
That kill in their sleep,

As I drew in my head,
Half-dazed and half-conscience,
Down he came,
Like an abominable man-monster,

Dressed in strange clothes,
From his head to his foot,
His teeth were all tarnished,
With darkness and soot,

From out of the shadows,
His eyes pierced my soul,
His gaze like a snake,
And his stare was so cold,

From the crack of his mouth,
He let forth a dark grin,
His voice filled the room,
Like a horrible sin,

Chained and racked,
Whipped to a stutter,
I barely heard his words,
And this he did utter,

"Make yourselves at home,
While we visit the coast,
You are my guest,
And I am your host,

Tonight you will dine,
On rot and insects,
And the rats from the depths,

Will feed on your flesh!

From the eyes of heaven,
To the pits of hell!
Tonight we sleep,
But tomorrow,
We set sail!"

In the mist of the morrow,
This they did sail,
Out into the unknown,
Toward an unspeakable hell!

The bottom of the ship's hull,
A human cargo-casket,
Have mercy on the souls,
That sailed the "Mid-Passage."

THE ELIAN

Achilles heel!
A sweet spot!
Ulysses arrogance,
Made Poseidon hot!

With hidden messages,
And many plots,
This stories a Banger!
Beware! Watch out!

So we turn the page,
To a hidden spot,
In little Havana,
Right down the block,

Didn't want to listen,
And couldn't cope,
So the media put them,
Under a microscope,

So adjust your lenses,
And up the light,
And let's take a look,
At Elian's Plight!

With friends and lawyers,
To his side,
Games, toys, tricks,
And vicious lies,

Mothers gone!
Decks stacked!
Father cries out,
"I want him back!"

Like a black hole,
Where gravity dwells,
The boy wants to stay,
Like a prisoner in hell,

So away they flew,
To make an appeal,
Judge got scared,
And said "OOPS! There it is!"

Like "Get Smart,"
With no intention to kill,
They found the house,
Like Jack found Jill,

The Grench stole Christmas,
What a fiendish plot,
They slammed on the brakes,

"Everyone Get Out!"

While rapping to Reno on the phone,
INS invaded our happy home,
Like jump out boys knocked down our
gate,
They came inside but it was too late!

A vision of blood,
Broke down our door,
They screamed they yelled,
"Everyone on the floor!"

A plan? A plot?
A hidden scheme?
Unpleasant, distasteful,
A most fiendish scene!

Someone yelled,
"We're under fire!"
Those political figures,
Just bold face liars!

The crowd outside,
Hot and mad,
Don't think about touching,
Our "Castaway Lad!"

With guns loaded,
And fingers cocked,
"Move out our way,
Or you will get clocked!"

So they yelled, they screamed,
They didn't hear,
Couldn't understand,
'The System's Basic Fear!'

So ashes to ashes,
And dust to dust,
This trilogy is a story,
From you to us,

So let all those,
Who oppose Mighty's Might,
Beware this story,
Of Elian's Plight!

UP TO HEAVEN AND DOWN TO HELL

Lizard and rodents!
Rodents and rats!
What can you tell me,
About that that that?

So up to heaven!
And down to hell!
There are a lot of things,
I can tell,

From whence they came,
A cold and barren place,
Our men they killed,
And our women they raped,

They killed! They raped!
They pillaged! They stole!
Let it be known,
Let the story be told,

A fly that buzzes,
Around and fast!
Come take a look,
Through the Looking-Glass,

From whence they came,

And them they sent,
Here's my story,
And the way it went!

Dr. Francis Cress,
Tried to help our nation,
She developed a theory,
Called "Color Confrontation,"

Martin Luther King,
And Malcolm X!
Our Nubian Kings,
In a rhyming text,

White Supremacy!
Like a box of Trix!
They shouted! They yelled,
"Blood can't be mixed!"

So up to heaven!
And down to hell!
Get ready and listen,
To a poet's tale,

Like the honey bee,
In Cheerios,
Let it be told!
Let the story unfold!

He stole Christmas,
Not a pleasant sight,
He came by day,
And slithered by night!

Like Lucky Charms,
It's magically delicious,
But education here,
It's not nutritious!

For seven days,
And seven nights,
And all I did,
Was fight! Fight! Fight!

Chains of victory,
Around my hand!
I might not win,
But maybe I can!

Thoughts of despair,
In my mind,
Transforming dreams,
Reality and time,

Like General Mills,
We eat, we like,
Beware our power!

Beware our light!

Can you see?
What I see,
My mind is busy,
As a bee!

So up to heaven!
And down to hell!
What can I do,
To break this spell?

A TALENT FOR VIOLENCE

Alien beings from a dying culture! Desti-
nation! Africa! Their mission? "To make it
their world." "We Come In Peace" was the
book that was given. But little did we
know as they stood on the shores and
watched their kings and queens taken to
distant lands, one deci-phered the "Book
of Peace" to reveal a hidden agen-da of
destruction! On the menu: Enslavement! It
read:

Day by day,
And night by night,
Let none of your people,
Escape my sight,

I will divide your culture,
And take your land,
Now try to catch me,
If you can?

Let those I enslave,
Feel my might,
Beware my power,
My deceptive light!

VIRTUES OF LIFE

Earth is the cultivation of wisdom. Wind is
freedom in its purest form. Fire is good
health manifesting itself. Soul is the water
that cleanses our inner-self. Wisdom is
common sense, the use of knowledge, and
our past experiences. Freedom is the uni-
verse around us and our movement
through it. Good health is spiritual, men-
tal, and physical wellness. Inner peace is
virtues of self-love, humble-ness, talent,
identity, respect, a-wareness of the uni-
verse and all life-forms that dwell in it.

I KNOW

I know where they've hidden the eyes of
Garret Morgan and Latimore's intrinsic
light!

At the stroke of midnight, like the galactic
eyes of god looking down upon us! I know!

Atlantis! Submerged in the pages of
colorful and artistic rhetoric left to the
imagination of a child's mind! But beware!
Prince Namor guards it well!

Some call him Dr. Strange! The mystic
sorcerer cloaks the Mind's Eye deep
within his Amulet of Armageddon! The
secret to his destruction "Lies In Love!"

POEM OF REMEMBRANCE

Remember these immortal words. As he stood there...a soldier of solitude, a hero in his own right, gazing up into a dark yet brilliant starlit sky, ponder-ing his fate, he reflected and said to himself, I finally understand that as I get smaller and smaller in my world equal to the size of a grain of salt, that I will not cease to exist...but in a factual yet unseemly reality, I am becoming one with the universe. And within understanding his destiny, he smiles and is at peace with himself.

PAGE INTENTIONALLY LEFT BLANK

Lightning Source UK Ltd.
Milton Keynes UK
UKHW021847111019
351423UK00011B/873/P